amicus illustrated

MATH WORLD
MEASURE IT

BY BRIDGET HEOS   ILLUSTRATED BY KATYA LONGHI

Amicus Illustrated is published by Amicus
P.O. Box 1329, Mankato, MN 56002
www.amicuspublishing.us

Editor: Rebecca Glaser
Designer: Kathleen Petelinsek

Library of Congress Cataloging-in-Publication Data
Heos, Bridget, author.
 Measure it / by Bridget Heos ; illustrated by Katya Longhi.
    pages cm. — (Math world)
 Summary: "Kids in a classroom practice measuring favorite objects
they brought from home using different units of measurement and
comparing the objects"— Provided by publisher.
 Audience: K to grade 3.
 Includes bibliographical references and index.
 ISBN 978-1-60753-464-8 (library binding : alk. paper) —
 ISBN 978-1-60753-679-6 (ebook)
 1. Measurement—Juvenile literature. 2. Physical measurements—
Juvenile literature. I. Longhi, Katya, illustrator. II. Title.
 QA465.H466 2015
 530.8—dc23   2013034702

Printed in the United States of America at Corporate Graphics
in North Mankato, Minnesota.

10 9 8 7 6 5 4 3 2 1

ABOUT THE AUTHOR

Bridget Heos is the author of more than
60 books for kids and teens, including many
books for Amicus Illustrated and her recent
picture book *Mustache Baby* (Houghton
Mifflin Harcourt, 2013). She lives in Kansas City
with her husband and four children. Visit her
on the Web at www.authorbridgetheos.com.

ABOUT THE ILLUSTRATOR

Katya Longhi was born in southern Italy. She
studied illustration at the Nemo NT Academy
of Digital Arts in Florence. She loves to create
dream worlds in her illustrations. She currently
lives in northern Italy with her Prince Charming.

Our class brought favorite objects from home for show and tell. We get to display them on our class shelf. But Ms. Lima says we need to measure them first.

At our table, Brooks brought the first book he read by himself.

Libby brought a ribbon from her grandmother.

I brought a Valentine's Day pencil from my best friend.

And Travis brought the box his family's refrigerator came in.

First we measure with paper clips.

"They shouldn't overlap," Ms. Lima says. "And there shouldn't be gaps in between them."

Brooks' book is 8 paper clips wide. Libby's ribbon is 20 paper clips long. My pencil is 7 paper clips long. Travis runs out of paper clips! Then we notice something.

I raise my hand. "The paper clips are different sizes. My pencil is 7 paper clips long with these. But it's 4 paper clips long with these."

"You're right," says Ms. Lima. "Things like paper clips vary in size. That's why standard measurements like centimeters and inches were invented. They are always the same."

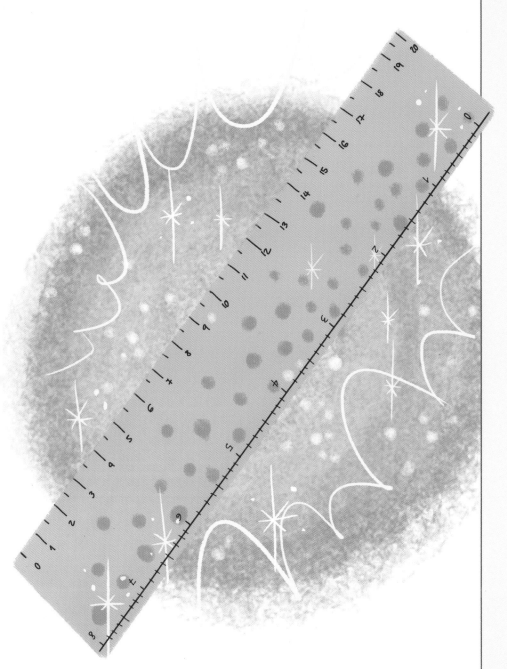

This time, Libby measures the ribbon with a ruler.

It is 21 inches long.

Brooks measures his book with a ruler. It is 21 centimeters tall. But Libby's ribbon looks longer than the book.

"Inches are bigger than centimeters," our teacher explains. "Let's all measure in centimeters."

At our table, we pretend our special things are in a family. Ribbon is the oldest. Book is second oldest Pencil is shorter than book. So it is also shorter than ribbon. "What about Travis' box?" Brooks asks.

53cm

21cm

15cm

"He is the giant that will eat the family!" Travis says. Our things are 218 centimeters all together.

129 cm

Our class lines up all of our special things by length.

My pencil is the same size as Alexa's mermaid.

"That means they're twins," Alexa says.

Altogether, our special things are 687 centimeters long. The shelf is only 150 centimeters long.

I have an idea. Each table can take a turn putting their things on the shelf.

687cm

Our table goes first.

But our items still don't fit.

"I guess there's only room for mine," Travis says.

"Travis!" we all say.

He takes something out of his pocket.

"Here, I brought something smaller. It's a stinger," Travis says.

He puts it on the shelf. It is less than a centimeter. We can barely see it.

"Though she be but little, she is fierce!" he says, pointing to where the bee stung him.

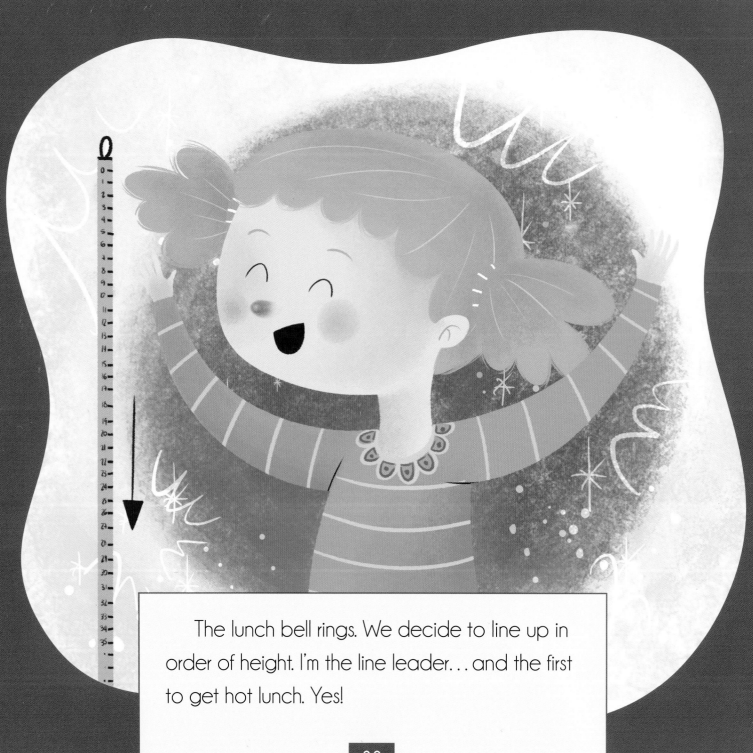

The lunch bell rings. We decide to line up in order of height. I'm the line leader... and the first to get hot lunch. Yes!

GLOSSARY

centimeter A standard metric unit, 100 of which make up a meter.

gap A space between two objects.

height The distance between the bottom and top of an object.

inch A U.S. standard unit, 12 of which make up a foot.

length A measurement of the longest side of an object.

measure To determine the size of something.

order The sequence of items organized in some way, such as by size.

overlap When an object covers another object.

"Though she be but little, she is fierce." A line from William Shakespeare's play, *A Midsummer Night's Dream*, meaning that something or someone can be small but also powerful.

READ MORE

Bussiere, Desirée. *What in the World is a Mile?: and Other Distance Measurements.* Minneapolis: ABDO Publishing Co., 2013.

Cleary, Brian. *How Long or How Wide?: A Measuring Guide* (Math Is Categorical). Minneapolis: Lerner, 2007.

Gunderson, Jessica. *How Long?: Wacky Ways to Compare Length.* North Mankato, Minn.: Picture Window Books, 2014.

Vogel, Julia. **Measuring Length.** Mankato, Minn.: The Child's World, 2013.

WEBSITES

BrainPOP: Measurement Movie
http://www.brainpop.com/science/scientificinquriry/measurement/
Watch Tim and Moby explain how measuring works.

California Division of Measurement Standards: Kids Corner
http://www.cdfa.ca.gov/dms/kidspage/kidsindex.htm
Read about the history of measurements, learn how to use the metric system, and ask the experts questions about measurements.

Measurement Games: PBS Kids
http://pbskids.org/games/measurement.html
Play measuring games featuring PBS characters to practice your math skills.

Every effort has been made to ensure that these websites are appropriate for children. However, because of the nature of the Internet, it is impossible to guarantee that these sites will remain active indefinitely or that their contents will not be altered.